Morpeth

Dear Mr. SWeeney

I Will always be grateful for all your hard Work teaching me and you will always be My favorite Male teacher! Here's a little book to remind you of 'Morpeth' and 'Sir Roberts School'

please see page 80

Love from
Tanara 🖤

"© crown copyright 1897"

Dear Mr. Sweeney,

Hope this book reminds you of your
visit & work in Morpeth.
I'm sure you'll be very familiar
with the photo's in this book.

All the very best for your
future.

Love,
Tamara & Salma x

(22/06/ 2014).

Then & Now
Morpeth

L.R. Mann and
W.M. Coulson

The History Press

Frontispiece: This map of Morpeth town shows extensive burgess plot developments behind the main streets and the Back Riggs area of the town in 1897. This map is a Crown copyright 1897 map for which acknowledgement goes to the Ordnance Survey.

First published in 2005 by Tempus Publishing

Reprinted in 2009 by
The History Press
The Mill, Brimscombe Port,
Stroud, Gloucestershire, GL5 2QG
www.thehistorypress.co.uk
© The late L.R. Mann and W.M. Coulson, 2005

The right of L.R. Mann and W.M. Coulson to be identified as the Authors of this work has been asserted in accordance with the Copyrights, Designs and Patents Act 1988.

British Library Cataloguing in Publication Data.
A catalogue record for this book is available from the British Library.

ISBN 978 0 7524 3582 4

Series design and typesetting by Liz Rudderham.
Origination by Tempus Publishing Limited.
Printed and bound in Great Britain.

Contents

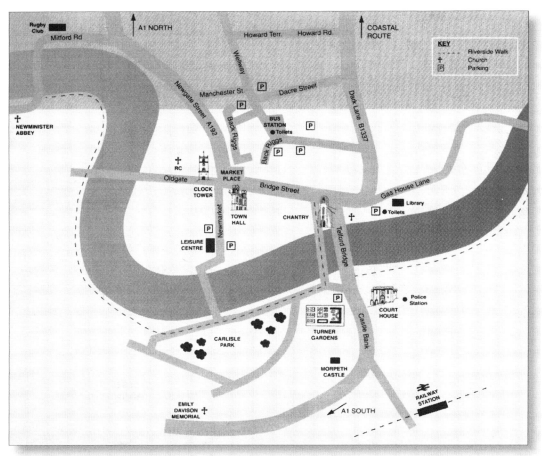

Street key map. (From Castle Morpeth Borough Council.)

Acknowledgements

*T*his book was written on behalf of the Morpeth Antiquarian Society, whose archives and collections have been plundered for old photographs. We particularly thank Mrs Janet Brown and Mrs Joan Taylor for their co-operation in locating our requests.

The early history of the town, starting in 1199 during the reign of King John, is not recorded on film; therefore, our photographs are from the 1850s onwards. We have relied on historical research by the late A.H. Tweddle. The data derived from his *Town Trails* publications, dating from 1983, has since been brought up to date in the comments on the following pages.

Our thanks are due to the many residents who contributed photographs and information during the preparation of this book, including the following;

Mr J. Alder, Mr D. Cockburn, Mrs N. Green, Mr T. Hackett, Mr R. Hawkins, Mr J. Landles (deceased.), Mr I. McCaffery, Revd R. McClean, Mr D. Murphy MP, Freeman Miss I. Smail OBE, Mr A. Swaile JP MBE, Cllr D. Thompson, Mrs G. Tym, Mr G. Jennings and Mr P.R. Carling BSc, who has assisted in the completion of this book.

L.R. Mann, OBE, CEng and W.M. Coulson ARIBA (retired)
(L.R. Mann died before the completion of this book.)

Introduction

Morpeth is a Northumberland town with a population today of about 15,000. Situated in a wooded valley, about fifteen miles north of Newcastle, it is on the old Great North Road and main railway line to Edinburgh. Every road into the town descends a hill.

A walk from one end of the town to the other, along the riverbank on an early summer morning, can be a delight. The fact that Morpeth is a very attractive place cannot have gone unnoticed by the growing number of incoming residents.

It is thought that the town has not always been in its present location, but half a mile south. A settlement may have existed there, centred on the medieval church of St Mary the Virgin. Archaeologists believe there is evidence of an earlier Anglo-Saxon church on the site. Certainly, the situation of Morpeth Castle would support this belief. Was this settlement called Kirkhill, today the name of a nearby housing estate?

Before the town was bypassed, Morpeth had been a vital staging post for travellers taking the east coast route between England and Scotland for centuries. The River Wansbeck, though not a significant watercourse, needed an all-weather crossing for the North Road; a hump-backed medieval bridge served this purpose until 1831. Now the base for a footbridge, the remains are prominent and adjacent to the preserved Chantry Chapel, a listed building which today houses a museum and commercial outlets. Traffic now crosses the Wansbeck on an elegant Thomas Telford bridge, which carries loads that the celebrated civil engineer would never have dreamed of.

For many years road travellers approaching from the north and south could read a roadside sign saying 'Welcome to Morpeth, Ancient Market Town'. Ancient it is. King John granted a charter for Morpeth's weekly market in 1199. In the late eighteenth century it was said to be the biggest 'fat market' outside Smithfield in London. Cattle and sheep were driven in their thousands from north Northumberland and from over the Scottish border. Escorted by drovers along drove roads and highways, livestock would take several days to converge on Morpeth for the weekly sale. Much of it was destined for consumption in the conurbations of Tyne and Wear, cities in the Midlands and even London itself. Cattle, sheep, pigs and poultry were held in pens from the top of Newgate Street to the bottom of Bridge Street, both part of the Great North Road! The air would be filled with animal noises and the cobbles covered with what they left behind. In addition, there was a corn and a butter market. In 1832 over 200 cattle and 2,500 sheep and lambs were being sold every week. Inevitably, there were links with several Morpeth tanneries and hide processors. Although the railway reached Morpeth in 1847 the practice of livestock trading in the main streets continued for many more years. A cattle mart near the station closed in 1985.

The combination of livestock marketing, catering for drovers and market traders and provision for travellers and carters must have had a considerable influence on the sort of town that Morpeth was in the nineteenth century. One feature which may have surprised a stranger was the presence of so many licensed premises. At one time over thirty could be found; Morpeth had more inns and hostelries per head of population than most towns of its size. They stood in ranks on each side of the road.

A prominent feature of the town's layout, clearly seen from an aerial photograph of Morpeth before the Second World War, was the network of alleys, lanes and burgess running at right angles from both sides of the two main streets. Now largely gone, some crowded parts of these living quarters had, in the nineteenth century, become notorious for unsanitary and disease-spreading habitation. Vestiges of this 'street plan' remain and are being conserved today by repaving the surviving alleys.

The fact that any significant coal deposits lie outside the town boundary, and that local workings were relatively small means that Morpeth carries few scars of industrial development. Apart from corn grinding and cloth finishing, which were done in several mills, tanning (done in several tan yards and polluting local water courses) and black-smithing, the only major manufacturer was Swinneys Engineering who were an important employer; the works produced a varied range of articles and machinery. The business, which grew to be a 'high-tech' affair, is said to have grown from a foundry based on a deposit of excellent moulding sand.

Horticulture and market gardening were widespread throughout Morpeth. Before fertile acres were taken for housing, produce grown for the neighbourhood and Tyneside was cared for by dozens of men and women. Commercial garden sites were in every corner of the town, and the names of the growers are remembered in the names of many streets and roads.

In the mid-nineteenth century Morpeth had a strong church-going population, a fact borne out by a church-going census of that time. Today there is still evidence of the many places of worship, and although some of the premises were converted to other uses they remain (alongside those that survive for their original purpose) and add considerably to a varied architectural scene.

The town, with its castle and nearby Cistercian abbey, has a long history of feudal patronage. The important craft guilds are remembered by the Town Hutch – a massive oak casket in which all money and parchments relating to the town's rights and affairs, and the records of the seven Craft Guilds of Morpeth were kept – and (more recently) by in-pavement plaques to be found in the attractively remodelled Market Place. The Civil War resulted in the siege of Morpeth Castle, and the scars are said to be visible on the gatehouse walls. Names of worthies with a local connection include Admiral Lord Collingwood, suffragette Emily Davison and botanist and herbalist William Turner.

Morpeth is Northumberland's county town, notwithstanding the claims of Alnwick, twenty miles to the north. Apart from the opinions of Morpethians, the claim to the title is supported by the building of the Northumberland County Council offices and Council Chamber to the south of the town. This administrative centre for the county was opened in 1982 by Prince Charles, and is architecturally very pleasing.

The preservation of Morpeth's history has occupied the interests of many researchers, conservationists and archivists. It has brought about the foundation of the local history group called The Morpeth Antiquarian Society, which has a strong association with this publication.

What is there for a visitor to Morpeth to see? There is no shortage of local history books on Morpeth. Like all such publications though, there can be a problem with them becoming dated. Visitors wanting to learn something of the town and its history can follow a signed route which, with a printed guide, will tell of some of the features to be seen. One series of publications worthy of study by someone wanting to learn about Morpeth and its past is Alec Tweddle's *Town Trails*. Written in instalments they criss-cross the town in a series of walks, and tell its history in detail.

A publication like *Morpeth Then and Now* can inform the curious as to how much the townscape, the town's characters and its institutions have changed with time.

Note on the text: On each page the old image is printed large and the recent image is smaller.

1

The Town's Approaches

*T*he principal approaches to Morpeth are from Newcastle in the south, Alnwick in the north and Ashington in the east. Each approach has places of interest shown on the following pages.

This page shows the fourteenth century parish church of St Mary the Virgin, on what was the A1 from Newcastle. St Mary's was once in the heart of the settlement but became isolated after the town moved down to the river. The Chantry was used as a Chapel of Ease until the church of St James the Great was consecrated in 1846. The 1861 lych-gate was built in memory of A.R. Fenwick of Netherton. The path was raised well above street level to keep worshippers away from the muddy road. The suffragette Emily Wilding Davison, who died in 1913 after stepping in front of the King's horse at the Derby, is buried here, as well as First and Second World War servicemen, including a number of Polish men. The churchyard is now full and a new cemetery was opened at Fairmoor in February 2003 by the Borough Council.

*C*oming from Newcastle to Morpeth on what used to be the A1, the traveller would have passed Catchburn Farm before coming to a series of large houses on the right-hand side. The first of these was Southgate. It was built in around 1900 for Colonel Gillespie, who at a different time also owned Greystoke (now a doctor's surgery).

In 1960, Southgate (and its extensive grounds) was taken over by the Civil Defence Corps as a training area and a number of 'bomb damaged' houses were built for rescue practice. The circular plaque on the van reads 'British War Relief Society – USA to Great Britain'.

At the beginning of the 1990s the site was cleared and seventeen houses and three bungalows were built. They were sizeable by modern standards, but still replaced only one original house. The development was named Southgate Wood.

*M*orpeth had a hospital with eight beds at Abbey House, Bullers Green from 1898. It was called the Victoria Cottage Hospital and Nurses Home, and was paid for by subscriptions from societies and local firms. It was replaced in 1910 by Wansbeck House (now Purdy's House) at the foot of Dogger Bank.

The present Cottage Hospital opened in 1932 with two wards and staff accommodation above. There were eleven beds for patients. The building was paid for by public subscription. It was taken over by the National Health Service in 1948 and considerable development has since taken place. A geriatric ward opened in 1968 and a sixty-bed extension opened in 1969. A three-storey building at the back of the original hospital includes an occupational therapy unit. The hospital now has three wards, an outpatients department and other specialist facilities, with eighty-four beds; it is run by the Northumbria Healthcare NHS Trust.

The Sun Inn is also on the southern approach road, just below St Mary's Church. The picture was taken in the 1920s, but the inn is believed to date back to 1798. It has had a long association with sporting events organised by the landlords – ranging from sparrow shooting to golf. Before the Morpeth Golf Club built its own clubhouse in 1910, the Sun Inn served the need, albeit unofficially.

The raised pavement and cottages were gradually removed in the 1930s for the road junction into the St Mary's Field housing estate, and in 1939 for the creation of the inn's car park. The building was refaced with artificial stone in 1990 and enlarged to occupy the adjoining house. This enabled the creation of an upstairs meeting room, which is well used by local groups.

The gateway to Carlisle Park stands opposite the courthouse. The parkland of thirty-three acres was given to the town by the Countess of Carlisle in 1916. It was planted and officially opened in 1929 by her great-grandson, the twelfth Earl of Carlisle. The planting, including the layout of paths and lawns, cost £500.

The gates and pillars were presented by Alderman W. Duncan in 1929. One gate bears the coat of arms of the Earls of Carlisle and the other the coat of arms of Morpeth, which was granted in 1552 and based on the 1255 seal of Sir Roger de Merley III. On it is Morpeth's motto 'Inter Sylvas et Flumina Habitans' (Dwelling between Woods and Waters).

Carlisle Park recently benefited from a £1.7million refurbishment, funded by the Heritage Lottery Fund. The work included the creation of the Turner Garden, which celebrates the sixteenth-century Morpeth-born herbalist William Turner. The park has also won a rare Green Flag Award for outstanding public spaces.

The road leading to the Telford bridge is viewed from Carlisle Park bank, before the building of the park keeper's house and the entrance gates in 1929. The imposing

courthouse, designed by John Dobson, is on the right. It formed the entrance to the county gaol, with its high walls and prison buildings behind. The gaol opened in 1829 and was in use until 1881; the courthouse continued to be used as such until 1980.

The small toll house on the left of the bridge approach was built to collect tolls to pay off the debt for the construction of the bridge and was used from 1832 until 1848. Opposite the toll house is Orde House. The growth of the trees somewhat mars the up-to-date picture, but it does show the park keeper's house and the top of the park gates.

Orde House, or No. 1 Pethgate, stood on the corner of Goose Hill and the main road. It was built in 1715 for Mr Orde, governor of the House of Correction that preceded the county gaol. The building was in fact two houses, one facing west and the other north, with large gardens behind stretching down to the river.

In 1912, the building was bought by Mr T. Robson. In 1920, Mr S. Waters and Mr Robson set up the mineral water company Waters & Robson in the Chantry Chapel building. The company moved to a new factory building in the garden of Orde House in 1937, then to the Coopies Lane industrial estate in the 1980s.

Mr Waters' sons set up Waters Bros as a garage business in the space between Orde House and the Telford bridge.

The house was sold to Adams & Gibbon in 1960. It was demolished in 1967 to build a new garage, car showroom and petrol sales forecourt. The garage is now owned by Davidsons of Morpeth.

The Newcastle & Berwick Railway reached Morpeth in 1847. Amalgamation quickly caused it to be renamed as the York, Newcastle & Berwick Railway, then the North Eastern Railway in the 1850s, and the London & North Eastern Railway in 1922. It is now the East Coast Main Line. Morpeth once had much more to offer. The Blyth & Tyne line provided an alternative route to Newcastle via Hepscott and Bedlington, and until 1880 it had its own Morpeth station, shown on the photographs, where Green (Agriculture) stands today.

The North British Railway also served Morpeth, linking it via the Wanney Line

to Rothbury and Reedsmouth. Prior to 1872, a line left the Blyth & Tyne track at Barmoor Junction and crossed over the North Eastern line at high level to join the Wanney line by today's golf course. As that required trains to reverse into or out of Morpeth Station, there were thoughts of building a third Morpeth station, presumably at Stobhill.

The Wanney Line left the main north-south railway line just south of Morpeth Station, at the start of the infamous Morpeth curve. The line from Morpeth to Scots Gap opened in 1862 and was extended to Reedsmouth Junction by 1865. From there it was possible to connect with trains to Edinburgh.

Trains from Morpeth to Reedsmouth called at Meldon, Angerton, Middleton, Scots Gap, Knowesgate and Woodburn. The line was never intended as a route from Morpeth to Edinburgh, but to serve the needs of agriculture along its length. The demise of the line in 1966 was greeted with sadness

– this was *our* special railway line! The final train – from Morpeth to Woodburn and back – was a Round Table charity excursion. Dubbed 'The Wansbeck Piper', the eleven-coach train was filled to capacity. As it left Woodburn, a piper played a lament.

In the 1960s picture (top), a steam train has just left the main line for Scots Gap. The modern picture shows the 50mph speed limit on the Morpeth Curve, with the tail-end of a Virgin train heading south.

The cattle market was a vital part of Morpeth life from early times. However, the practice of holding it in Bridge Street eventually became unacceptable, and in 1903 a new market was created behind the town hall, with access through Grey's Yard in Oldgate until a new street, called Newmarket, was opened in 1927.

The arrival of the railway led to the opening of two other cattle markets, one on each side of the Stobhill Road, just to the south of the railway bridge. The smaller one, on the west

side of the road, closed in the 1940s. After the Newmarket mart was closed in 1956, the market pictured (which was adjacent to the station) was the only cattle market left in Morpeth. The site was sold for housing development and the Carlisle Lea estate was built in 1985. Today the site of the cattle pens is part of Kingswell, the road through the estate. The old Blyth & Tyne railway buildings are visible in the background.

The YMCA building was located at Damside on Dark Lane, with a tennis court on the frontage. It was formerly a parochial hall used by the Church Institute for social functions and meetings of the Boys' Brigade, Girl Guides and many other groups. In 1939 the YMCA ran a service canteen for troops stationed in the area, which was well appreciated. By 1983 the membership of the YMCA had dwindled, making them unable to maintain the property. It therefore closed and the site was sold to a developer.

Before demolition, ground investigation on the tennis court area revealed evidence of a timber building, which was the workshop of the sawmill marked on the 1897 Ordnance Survey map. The building was demolished in September 1999 and the site was redeveloped with twenty-four private apartments in two multi-storey blocks, known as Admiral Lord Collingwood Court.

The East Mill is a Grade II listed building on the Pegswood road. A 1566 document indicates that it was established by the Lord of Morpeth to aid the Town Mill further upstream, which has appeared on maps since 1604 (see chapter five). Originally a three-storey water mill, a large four-storey building (bearing the inscription 'New Process Flour Mills 1892') was added by W. Davison, who converted the mill to be driven by steam

power. Finally, the three-storey miller's house was added. The premises were sold to the Milburn Estate in 1914 and were then used as a factory for the production of goods including Andrews Liver Salts and powdered egg for the Ministry of Food.

The millrace, which is still visible, drove the wheel connected to the millstones and a hoist for lifting corn sacks. The 1920s photograph was taken from the opposite riverbank, which could not be achieved today.

2

Bridge Street

*B*ridge Street is one of the two main shopping streets in Morpeth at the time of writing. What changes may occur in the very near future is still a matter of speculation. The picture shows what is today just the side entrance to the Sanderson Arcade. However, it predates the arcade by some fifty years, having been the entrance to the post office.

If the proposed total redevelopment of the Back Riggs takes place it is likely to be swept away, along with the arcade itself.

When the cattle market was in its heyday Bridge Street would have been a hive of activity, with cattle along the street and buyers and sellers to be found in the several hostelries that catered for the needs of weary travellers.

ooking from the Chantry towards Market Place, this early view of Bridge Street on market day allows us to look mainly at the south side of the street. The absence of the mock-Tudor facing on what used to be Appleby's shop is noticeable, being the first building on the left. Next door to Appleby's at No. 48 stood Vose's Refreshment Rooms, built in 1888 for Alderman Gray, who was mayor in 1876 and again in 1906. Septimus Jennings opened his cycle shop in this building in the early years of the twentieth century.

The town hall and the clock tower are visible in the background, as is Watson's Corner, seen before the building of the second YMCA building in the town. On the north side of the road the bow-fronted Black Bull Hotel can be seen, which dates from 1748. Today's view is very similar, one notable difference being the pedestrian crossing with its traffic lights and zig-zag road markings.

BRIDGE STREET — MORPETH *G 9902*

This is a similar view of Bridge Street, taken at a later date – the cars, as well as people's dress, suggest the 1950s. There is talk today of Morpeth becoming gridlocked by traffic. The very surprising number of cars in this picture indicates that we have been close to it for quite a while!

Appleby's Corner is now adorned with its mock-Tudor facing. Note the car parked right beside the 'No Waiting' sign outside Appleby's. Little has changed since then with regard to parking. There is still no pedestrian crossing. Hopefully the man purposefully striding towards the Black Bull made it safely across the road.

On the right hand edge of the picture, a Tecalemit sign is clearly visible. It was on the wall of Jennings Garage. In the background, the second YMCA building is now to be seen. In the modern view, trees obscure Appleby's Corner. The Black Bull has been joined by Chambers as an alternative watering hole, and Jennings Garage has gone, to be replaced by Chantry Mews.

*L*ooking from Market Place towards St George's Church, it is just possible to make out the railings that used to surround the church. Daglish was an ironmonger, judging by the brooms hanging outside the window. Would they still be there if left outside today? Older sisters proudly display babies as they chat. The prams are rather different to those in use a century later. The shop next to Daglish's advertises that it is an 'Agent for Pullars Dye Works' in Perth. The Black Bull, beyond the lamp post, gives us our bearings.

Across the road, the large crested sign by the other lamp post is for Wight, the coachmaker. The protruding sign to the right of Wight's is for a tailor's shop. To the immediate left of Wight's is Davidson's druggists, sharing the building with J.H. Hudson. The cattle indicate that it is market day again – as does the manure on the street. The present day picture shows changes in shop owners and unsightly painted road markings.

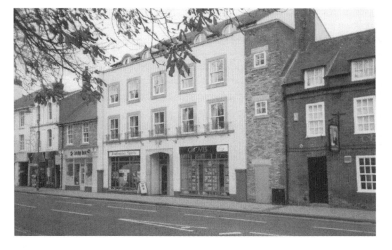

The premises of S. Jennings Ltd, at No. 55 Bridge Street, was a splendid eighteenth-century building which was occupied by Dr Skrimshire at the turn of the nineteenth century. He sold it in 1902. For a time it housed a fruit market, and from 1910 to 1912 it was a Temperance Hotel. It then stood empty until Septimus Jennings bought it in 1914 and converted the ground floor into a garage for eighty cars and a workshop employing thirteen people. In 1921 a petrol pump was installed on the pavement in front of the garage.

Jennings moved to Coopies Lane in 1996 and the Bridge Street building was sold for conversion into flats with three small shops at ground level. It was intended that the classical façade should be retained, but when alterations commenced the building was found to be unstable and it was demolished completely. In spite of worries at the time, the new building blends very well into its surroundings and is now called Chantry Mews, designed by architect Jane Darbyshire.

George Rutherford opened his drapery business at No. 10 Bridge Street in 1846, in premises that had previously housed the King's Arms inn. The drapery business thrived and expanded. In 1902, the family ceased to live over the shop and the upper floors were used for retail purposes. No. 12 was taken over later and Nos 14 and 16 were demolished in 1926 to make way for a new extension to the shop. No. 16 had been run as a millinery business for a time by George's daughter Ella. Today, Rutherford's occupies Nos 10-16 Bridge Street. In 1906 the firm also had premises at No. 36 to sell ladies underwear. From 1983 to 1994 they had a furniture shop in Oldgate, which is now Charlton's DIY store.

*P*roceeding from Rutherford's towards the town hall, after Woolworth's comes the Queen's Head Hotel. That hotel has been on the same site since around 1720. It is not illustrated as its external appearance has altered little over the past century. It is mentioned as it is the first of no less than five licensed premises that stood in a row, stretching to the town hall. Morpeth appears to have been exceptionally well-endowed with inns and hotels at the turn of the nineteenth century. They existed to cater for the thirsts of farmers and drovers who had travelled long distances to the market.

Next to the Queen's Head stood the King's Head, which existed from around 1764 until 1933, when it was declared redundant by the police. The building was demolished and replaced by the present bank building.

*N*ext door to the King's Head stood the Turk's Head, the third in our row of five hostelries on the approach to the town hall. All five were in use until 1916, when the Turk's Head was closed. It had been a hostelry from at least 1798. In 1822 the 'Wonder Coach' from Alnwick called here and carriers also plied their trade from here to Blyth, Newcastle and Wooler. In 1855, this inn was the base for the carrier to Elsdon and Otterburn. That same year it is described as having ten rooms, three attics, a kitchen, a bar, two cellars, a brewhouse, malt-loft, hop-loft, coach house, gig house, stalls for twenty-one horses, two warehouses, a joiner's shop, blacksmith's shop, soot-house, pig-houses and also six dwelling houses behind, between the inn and the Wansbeck, and a garden 22yd long and 5yd wide. The premises were rebuilt in 1939 and are currently occupied by Decoflair. The remains of a mounting block can still be seen in the pavement.

*F*rom the Turk's Head, the town hall was approached by passing the George & Dragon Hotel. It was operational in 1798 and remained so until its closure in 1973, having been rebuilt in 1907. In 1829 it was advertised for sale with ten rooms, a bar, cellar, garret, a six-stalled stable and a blacksmith's shop. Also there was a large brewery, two rooms above a malt mill, ale and porter cellars, a cooper's shop, office, granary and seven-stalled stable, a garden and a summerhouse. Clearly it was a business of some importance.

There was also an inn within the George & Dragon Yard, called the Board Inn, but its licence was not renewed in 1939 – it could scarcely have been needed by then. Today, the premises are occupied by Etam PLC, a fashion shop.

*T*he final watering hole in the (perhaps by now unsteady) walk to the town hall was the Earl Grey Hotel. Opened in around 1834, it changed hands for £1,250 in 1869 and again in 1897 for £5,500, at which time it is reported as having six bedrooms and stalls for fourteen horses, as well as a smithy. It is recorded that in 1882 'a horse and conveyance met every train' and that it was a popular haunt for local cycling clubs later in that decade.

Carriers operated from the hotel, with regular services to Netherton and Whittingham recorded in 1855 and to Monkseaton and Bedlington in 1890. The hotel was rebuilt in 1931, but the horse-mounting block was still in place on the pavement until 1960. The hotel closed in 1973, when the then Abbey National Building Society moved into the premises, with the upper floor now being the offices of the Town Council, right next to the town hall.

3

Market Place, Newmarket and Oldgate

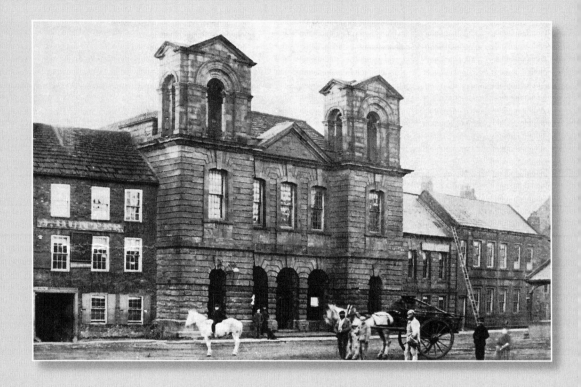

M arket Place is the heart of the town, where the weekly market was held. In fact, the market spread right along Bridge Street and also up Newgate Street. The most imposing building in Market Place is the town hall, shown in the 1920s. The original building was designed by Sir John Vanburgh for the Earl of Carlisle in 1714. After a fire in 1869 it was rebuilt retaining the Vanburgh stone façade, but with the other walls rebuilt in brick.

Inside the entrance is the butter market, and beyond that the corn exchange. The stone staircase leads up to the ballroom, the old Council Chamber – which contains the Town Hutch and five of the seven Guild Boxes – and the mayor's parlour, with countless civic treasures. Notable among these are the 1604 Mace and the Charter of Incorporation granted by Charles II in 1662.

The buildings to the right of the town hall were demolished in around 1925 to allow construction of the Newmarket access road.

The low building on the corner of Oldgate and Market Place was known as Watson's Corner. The picture was taken in the 1890s, obviously on market day. The building dated from around 1675. Along with other property owned by Alderman Bainbridge, it was demolished in 1905 and replaced by the town's second YMCA building. The ground floor has shops that extend round the corner into Oldgate, but the upper floors were occupied by the YMCA until 1952, when the YMCA moved to the parochial hall on Dark Lane. Today the upper floors are used by the Manzil restaurant and residential flats.

The detached clock tower is a rarity in England. Standing 65ft high, it was built in around 1578 from re-used medieval stone, probably taken from the ruins of Newminster Abbey. The top storey was added in 1705 to house a peal of six bells given by Major General Main, MP for Morpeth. The cattle market moved from Market Place into Newmarket in 1903

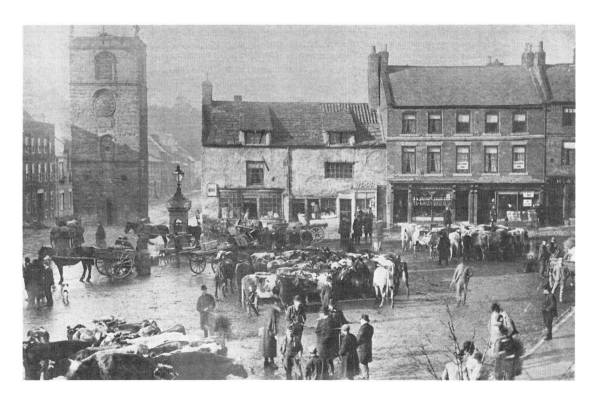

*L*ooking east across Market Place, the 1920s view along Bridge Street was taken on a quiet summer day, with the shop awnings extended. There are no cars, just the United bus and a van. Quite a contrast to today.

On the left is the Playhouse cinema, built in 1915 to replace earlier shops. It closed in 1961 and the building was taken over by Laws Stores. The building was given a new brick frontage in 1982. The ground floor was then occupied by Iceland, with Gianni's Pizzeria taking over the upper floor. The building behind the bus became unsafe and was rebuilt in a traditional style in 1982 for the Newcastle Building Society.

Market Place was given a considerable facelift in 2003, being paved with large York stone slabs. The pavement includes a row of cast metal plaques to commemorate the seven craft guilds of the town, which date from 1417. The companies were; Cordwainers; Weavers; Smiths, Saddlers & Armourers; Skinners, Glovers & Butchers; Tanners; Fullers, Dyers, Curriers & Hatters; and Merchants & Tailors, all formed by the joining of twenty-four former separate guilds in 1523, or thereabouts.

*L*ooking up Newgate Street from the town hall in the mid-1920s, the dominant feature is the Hollon Fountain. It was erected in 1885, carved from granite blocks and paid for by public subscription to thank R.W. Hollon for an annuity given in memory of his wife Mary. The annuity provided a token income for deserving residents, as well as a meat tea at a local inn. There are some eighty annuitants still being supported.

The fountain came to be used as an unofficial traffic island and its location was a source of controversy until a vehicle demolished it in 2002. As part of the 2003 redevelopment of Market Place the road layout was revised and the Hollon Fountain re-erected in front of the clock tower, out of harms way. The awning on the left of the picture is Dance & Carr's café, located in Bridge Street at one time. Today it has been replaced by Greenwood the Outfitter, who are now closing down.

The Liberal Club stood next to Watson's Corner in the late 1880s and until at least 1893. The building was demolished in 1904. On its left was the 'Shaving & Hair Cutting Establishment' of Mr A. Wilson. The shop of Mr C. Middlemiss was a 'Grocers and Provision Merchants'. The name 'Jubilee Shop' probably refers to Queen Victoria's Golden Jubilee in 1887, dating the picture to that year. Note the name Middlemiss. In the next chapter will be found the house furnisher G.W. Middlemas. Despite the spelling variation, both men belonged to the same family.

To the right of the Liberal Club, the business of Chirney & Egdell was probably a grocery;

T.J. Chirney was a grocer in Newgate Street in 1879 and H.J. & M.J. Egdell were grocers at 1 Newgate Street in 1897. Was Mr Chirney, the shopkeeper, related to G.B. Chirney, mayor of Morpeth in 1883?

The door at the left of the shop led to the premises of John Brown, a seedsman. It is now shown as another charity shop in the town.

Admiral Lord Collingwood had his home in Oldgate from 1791 until his death in 1810. Inset into the picture is a copy of the plaque that was erected above the front door by the Corporation of Morpeth in 1905 to mark the importance of the house. There was an extensive garden and orchard behind the house. This was purchased by Father G.A. Lowe for the building of St Robert's Church, which opened in 1850. After that a school was built to the right of the house.

The modern picture reveals that the cottage that stood to the left of Collingwood's house has been demolished, but left its mark on the house. The space is now occupied by the church car park entrance. The house is now part of St Robert's presbytery. A new entrance has been made on the side of the building, and the original front door is no longer in use.

*P*rior to the establishment of Newmarket in 1903, market gardens stretched from the back of the town hall to the river wall. The tower of St James' Church, completed in 1852 (six years after the completion of the church), is very visible in the background. The alleyway next to the town hall passed under the Scotch Arms Inn. It was demolished to allow construction of the road (Newmarket) built to allow better access to the new market area, which had been opened to clear livestock from Market Place.

Newmarket had pens to hold 1000 cattle and sheep and did a thriving business until 1957, when the cattle market was moved to Stobhill. The road looks very different today. The Coliseum cinema, on the left, was built in 1927. It ceased to operate as a cinema in the 1990s and is now a nightclub. The modern building on the right is called Fountain House, containing the Job Centre and the County Court.

Oldgate was quieter in the nineteenth century – with swans sitting in the road! The post office is on the right of the picture, with a sign indicating that it had a public telephone inside. As far back as 1677, the postmaster of Morpeth operated from Oldgate, although originally from Old Queen's Head Yard on the opposite side of the road.

Admiral Collingwood's house is seen on the right with two chimneystacks, but the cottage to the left is now demolished. The house in the distance that appears to be in the middle of the road is actually on the other side of the river, and has been occupied by the Morpeth Social Club since 1954. The recent picture emphasises the change in traffic, with bollards protecting the clock tower from damage. Also prominent is the Crown post office, opened in 1968 but now used only as a Royal Mail delivery office.

4

Newgate Street

*N*ewgate Street starts at Market Place, going north for a quarter of a mile to Bullers Green where it divides, one road west to Mitford and the other north onto the old turnpike road to Scotland. A map of 1826 marks the lower section 'Newgate' and the upper half 'Silver Street' from Copper Chare. We don't know why, unless the residents were wealthier!

The photograph shows Beeswing House, located on the west side at No. 93. This unique property with a quadrant corner and shop doorway in fine ashlar is named after a racehorse that won twenty-four gold cups for its owner William Orde, of Nunnykirk. The building was a public house until 1871 and then a general shop, becoming derelict before purchase by Mr K. Green, who improved it for an antiques shop. In 1984 it was sold to Mr T. Glendenning, a vintner, for his trade. Before the by-pass road was built in 1970 all A1 traffic passed up Newgate Street, which contained many inns.

Looking down Newgate Street, a sign next door to Schofield's pharmacy indicates that Dance & Carr offered refreshments. They were also at 4 Market Place (Greenwoods) and at 13 Newgate Street (Pattinsons) in the early 1900s. Further down, the Nag's Head Inn is where T. & G. Allan stands today.

Across the road in the foreground, No. 29 is a substantial early-eighteenth century house to the north of Bakehouse Yard. There are still bakery ovens in the cellars. Over the years the building has had many uses, including a bank, a working men's club, a gentlemen's club, a surgery and a tax office. Originally the arches were open, but windows were inserted by Lance Robson, an estate agent, in around 1960 and the building was renamed Robson House. The gentlemen in conversation in the middle of the road show the lack of traffic in those days and would be in some danger today.

The modern picture shows little change apart from the replacement of the Nag's Head by T. & G. Allan and the windows in the archways of Robson House.

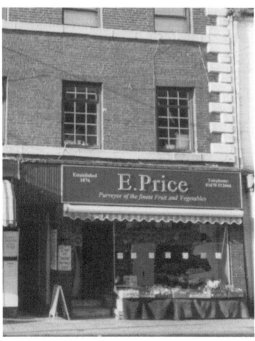

No. 9 Newgate Street is a shop that was once owned by G.W. Middlemas, a household furniture supplier in the early 1900s. Signs proclaim that he was noted for bedsteads, fenders and firebrasses. The property is a solidly built late-eighteenth century town house with a shop below and a side passage leading through to the back of the premises.

Today the property is owned by E. Price, a greengrocer who has traded on this site for at least seventy years. The facia board states that the business was established in 1876. It is known that the family were once market gardeners in the town, so perhaps the shop was opened later as an outlet for their produce.

Schofield's chemists shop was at 32 Newgate Street. The picture was taken in the 1920s and, judging by the open door and windows, it was taken in summertime. The three-storey building dates back to the late eighteenth century and has been a pharmacy since 1838, when the business was established by Mr J. Hood. Mr Schofield bought the business in 1877, and later it was owned by a Mr Marshall.

By the 1950s the business had been sold to Alec Sim, whose wife's maiden name was Webb. Although Mrs Sim was not active in the business, it was named Sim & Webb and that name still appears above the entrance. The business has changed hands at least three times since Mr Sim retired. For the past few years it has belonged to Moss Chemists, who own two other pharmacies in the town.

*N*o. 16 Newgate Street is on the east side of the road, below the Nag's Head Inn (now T.G. Allen's). The picture shows that it was Jobsons' Cocoa Rooms in the 1920s, in a three-storey eighteenth-century property with offset dormer windows. This later became Robson's Café until 1974, when it was taken over by Charles Harrison as an outdoor clothing and school outfitters shop. The Harrison business was begun by Robin Harrison in 1921 at No. 53 Newgate Street. His son Charles moved to No. 16 and retired in 1999, when the building was occupied by Age Concern as a charity shop (bringing the current total of charity shops in Morpeth to six). It was noticed that a good crop of grass is now growing in the roof gutters!

*L*ooking down Newgate Street from the north; this picture was taken in the 1930s. Was the absence of traffic due to the presence of two policemen standing in the middle of the road?

The Black & Grey Inn, which has existed since 1798, used to be called the Black & Grey Horses Inn, so the claim to 'Good Stabling' is not surprising. To the right is the narrow lane called Copper Chare, which appears on the 1821 map of the town. Beyond Copper Chare is the Co-operative building, erected at the beginning of the twentieth century. The window onto Copper Chare has the word

'Shoes' above it, giving a clue to at least one item offered for sale. The upper floor was a large hall used for dances, amongst other things. Since 1974 Econofreeze, who sell white goods, have occupied the building. The hall above is now used by a health club. The high wall on the right of the picture surrounded the workhouse, but was demolished when the telephone exchange was built.

*T*he Grey memorial arches fronting on to Newgate Street are at the west end of the avenue of lime trees leading to St James' Church. They were erected as a memorial to the rector Francis Grey after his death in 1890 and were designed by W.S. Hicks of Newcastle. The stone arches are supported by six twin pairs of Frosterley marble pillars. Wrought iron railings (made by Swinney Brothers) were set between the arches and a small garden was planted in front, up to the pavement. There is an inscription across the top, which reads: 'Lord I have loved the habitation of thy house and the place where thine honour dwelleth'.

Today's picture shows that the frontage kerb rails are now missing, having been taken to make shells during the Second World War. The garden frontage has been paved over and a memorial seat has been placed on each side of the gateway.

This picture of the workhouse at the top of Newgate Street was taken from across the river at the time it was being demolished in the 1950s. The substantial four-storey brick building was erected between 1866 and 1868 to house 150 inmates. It had a gatehouse and a high wall fronting onto the street.

The main building and staff house overlooked the river and High Stanners Park at the back. The workhouse ceased to be used in the 1930s and the inmates were relocated to the Thomas Taylor homes at Hepscott Park. From 1939 until 1943 the building was used by the County Treasurer's Department, which had been evacuated from Newcastle as a wartime safety measure.

A large (and at the time modern) telephone exchange was built on the site in 1963. It dominates the street frontage and must be a prime site for redevelopment. With the advent of computer-based equipment, the building must be considerably larger than is necessary for a telephone exchange today.

*T*he old Nag's Head Inn, described as the 'Grey Nag's Head Inn' in the picture, stood on the east side of Newgate Street from at least the 1770s and is thought to have been one of the oldest inns in the town. This early picture shows two gable ends on the frontage. At a later date, two smaller gable ends were added between them. At the rear there was a yard with stables that were used for farmers' horses on market days. During the eighteenth century carriers travelled between here and the villages of Cambo and Wingates.

The inn was demolished in the late 1960s and replaced with a modern two-storey building for T. & G. Allan, the stationers and booksellers. The new building has a flat stone façade, in contrast to the traditional properties on either side. The first floor of the shop was extended at the back in 2004 with an arched parapet over Nag's Head Yard, which links Newgate Street to the Back Riggs.

*N*os 37 and 39 Newgate Street were two shops with workshops attached. They were demolished in 1938 and the site was vacant until 2000, when, to tidy up the gap, two advertising hoardings were erected in a V shape, with a small gate between leading down to a private house at the back.

The site was cleared to create a way into Mains Place, a development of town houses and flats between Newgate Street and the river. The new archway, completed in 2000 and leading into the development from Newgate Street, was built by the Nomad Housing Group and contains eight flats. The archway also covers a small shop at ground level, currently occupied by an Italian delicatessen.

5

The River

The River Wansbeck meanders through the heart of Morpeth. The need to maintain water levels for the various mills that existed led to the construction of weirs, including those built to provide water for Oliver's Mill and the Lord's (or Town) Mill. To facilitate movement about the town stepping-stones were provided, notably at Bakehouse Yard. There were fords at Oldgate and Low Stanners and then a number of bridges were built, first to accommodate foot traffic and then vehicular traffic.

Today there are three footbridges and two vehicular bridges in the centre of town. The following pages will look at four of these. The footbridge joining Dogger Bank to the High Stanners is not depicted, but deserves a mention – built in 1904, it is having an unsung centenary year as this book is being written. It is known as Skinnery Bridge. The plaque depicted is attached to the footbridge beside the Chantry and indicates that the bridge was constructed by Swinney Bros, local engineers.

There was a medieval bridge carrying the main Edinburgh-Newcastle road across the Wansbeck beside the Chantry. However, it was deemed unsafe after a mail coach toppled over and fell into the river for the second time. A new bridge was built in 1831 and was subject to a toll charge. Human nature being what it is, steps had to be taken to prevent people avoiding the toll by continuing to use the old bridge. The problem was solved by the use of explosives to demolish it. However, the central pillar was left standing and, as the plaque indicates, used to support the footbridge that was erected in 1869, at a cost of £60.

The footbridge was extensively repaired in 2004 and provides a valuable shortcut for pedestrians from Castle Square into the town centre – well away from the busy main road traffic. Oliver's Mill is seen clearly in the background of the picture.

The second of the Oldgate bridges was recycled! Judging by the ice on the river, perhaps it found its original location a bit too cold. It is now at Low Stanners, at the foot of Borehole Lane. Following the collapse of the chain bridge, this lattice girder bridge was erected in Oldgate in 1830. It was only a footbridge and the demand from vehicular traffic rendered it obsolete by 1932, when it was replaced by a structure known as the 'Meccano Bridge', which was in use until 1970.

The lattice bridge was moved to Low Stanners in 1932. The bridge was placed on bogies and hauled to its new site by a steam tractor owned by R.T. & J. Hewitt, a Morpeth firm of haulage contractors. The present day picture shows the relocated bridge.

There was a need for a footbridge to join Carlisle Park to Newmarket, which was met by the construction of the original Elliott Bridge in 1925. The bridge was paid for by public subscription and opened by R. Elliott who was mayor at the time. It succumbed to the ravages of time and was replaced by the new Elliott Bridge in 1982. The new bridge was built two feet higher than the original to allow more space for floodwaters. It was opened by Sir William Elliott MP, later Lord Elliott, who was the son of the former mayor.

From 1958 until the 1970s, the Round Table held an annual regatta on this stretch of river. A variety of curious vessels took to the water with the object of pushing the crews of rival boats into the river. By today's standards, the event was highly unsafe – but it was great fun! In the summer, rowing boats can be hired to ply between Oldgate Bridge and the weir at Oliver's Mill.

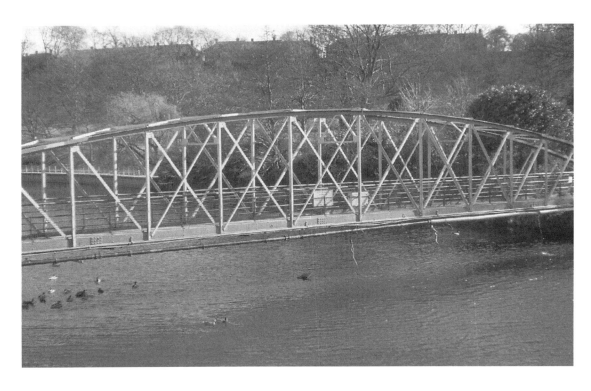

*B*akehouse Steps appear on the 1826 map of Morpeth but are much older than that, being referred to in the Bailiff's accounts for 1771. Some say that one is not a true Morpethian until one has fallen into the river from these steps. Still very much used by scholars on their way to and from school, it is interesting to note the safety concerns that have been expressed in recent times. They may well have been the cause of some wet feet but, so far as the writer is aware, they have caused no fatalities in over 200 years of known usage.

An earlier map, dated 1826, shows four sets of stepping-stones across the river at Bullers Green, Bakehouse, Oldgate and Goosehill. Today only the Bakehouse steps remain for use at low water by active residents. The steps join the High Stanners to Newgate Street. St Robert's Church, built in what was once Admiral Collingwood's back garden, forms a pleasant backdrop to the scene.

*T*his weir supplied water for Oliver's Mill. An earlier weir, about 100m downstream, supplied water to the Lord's (or Town) Mill, which stood on the present site of St George's United Reformed Church. Part of the millrace can still be seen under the floor of the church. Oliver's Mill was built in the eighteenth and nineteenth centuries and accommodated both a woollen mill and a corn mill. The business must have been profitable as the Olivers played a considerable part in the erection of the cottage hospital. Their portraits are to be found in the hospital. This mill was partially burned out before work was done in 1991 to convert it into the present block of flats by Nomad homes.

The Lord's Mill was still standing in 1856, but must have been demolished shortly afterwards to make way for the (then) Presbyterian church, which held its first service of worship on Thursday 12 April 1860. Note the floodwall in front of Oliver's Mill, built after the 1963 floods damaged some 460 houses.

6

Back Riggs

The Back Riggs area stretches from Bridge Street to Dacre Street and from Newgate Street to Dark Lane. It was a run-down area, overcrowded and unhygienic in parts, until it was gradually demolished between the 1930s and the 1970s. It was also home to Swinney Brothers, Morpeth's only large-scale engineering business. The area now includes the Sanderson Arcade, built in 1939, the bus station (which moved to the site in 1981) and the major stores of Morrison's (opened in 1986 as Safeway), Lidl (1996), the North East Co-op and smaller shops and car parks. There is talk, at the time of writing, of clearing the area again and replacing it with a modern shopping mall and housing. Some say that if the project goes ahead the character of Morpeth as a market town will be lost.

The picture is of a smithy which dates back to at least the eighteenth century and was occupied by the Boutflower family from around 1900 until 1974, when Jack Boutflower retired. The building was demolished in 1977. Behind is Sanderson's brewery, since demolished for Lidl's store.

J. & J.S. Mackay, printers, publishers and stationers, have had their shop at 19 Bridge Street since the 1860s. Prior to that it was the Old Hope & Anchor inn, owned by a family called McClelland. The pub and its outbuildings stretched back across the site. When Mackays bought the premises they set up a printing works that eventually occupied

all the buildings shown in the upper picture and extended beyond that. The *Morpeth Herald* was produced here from the 1860s until the 1980s. The single chimney, now demolished, vented the furnace that melted the printer's lead type.

In 1985 the old buildings to the right of the three-storey building were sold to David Hicks, who operates Town & Country Antique Furniture Restorers from there.

*T*he somewhat ramshackle building on the left was the workshop of T. Dunn, joiner, builder and shopfitter. Since 1975 the firm has operated as T. Dunn & Son, 'Builders of Residential and Commercial Property', from their Coopies Lane industrial estate offices.

The business was started by Tommy Dunn in 1960, with a bicycle. A van was soon acquired to transport materials, but in the early days employees walked to sites on which they were working. Early work included repairs to Smail's after the fire in 1969 and

various jobs for Rutherford's. The Back Riggs building stood in line with Mackay's and the Town & Country Antique Furniture Restorers, approximately where the Co-op loading bay is today. Prior to being occupied by Dunn's, the building, which was owned by the Borough Council, had been used as a bakery and was demolished during the 1970s clearances.

*L*oades Brewery stood in Union Street, opposite the entrance to Dacre Court. Built in 1863, it was in operation until the turn of the twentieth century. It would appear that the entire staff turned out for the picture. Was the child on the right also an employee? This brewery was one of no fewer than six breweries in Back Riggs. The largest was the Hope & Anchor Brewery, which stood approximately on the site of the filling station beside Lidl now. After the brewery closed the building found various industrial uses before it was demolished in 1937, and the site forms part of the car park today.

Albert Mears Loades lived in Kings Avenue but is believed to have emigrated to South Africa, where he ended his days.

This building stood at the northwest corner of Corporation Yard, where it met the Back Riggs – just a little to the north of Boutflower's Smithy. Perhaps it was typical of the housing in the area. Probably dating back to the eighteenth century, it would have been built as a dwelling house, but it was used as a chapel of rest towards the end of its life. Inevitably the local children referred to it as the 'Spooky House'.

The ladies standing beside the door were dressed typically for the times. Socially, they appear to be a cut above those ladies who are reputed to have sat on their doorsteps smoking clay pipes. The building was demolished in the 1970s clearance and the site is now occupied by the Co-op store.

This terrace of houses was built on Union Street in 1939 as the first wave of improvements in Back Riggs. They stood on the east side of the street (which does not exist today) near the corner of Back Riggs Lane. This terrace, along with other houses, was demolished in the 1970s clearances in the area. A new bus station was built on the terrace site in 1981 with an arched concourse and toilets to replace the open stands for passengers in Newmarket. The large bus-parking area has a space reserved for tour buses making a comfort stop in Morpeth, exactly as the stagecoaches did in the past. Morpeth Pride recently carried out grant-aided improvements to the bus station, now with glazed screens, to impress arrivals in the town, the work being completed in 2004 and opened by the mayor, Cllr Derek Thompson. It has now been demolished for Back Riggs redevelopment.

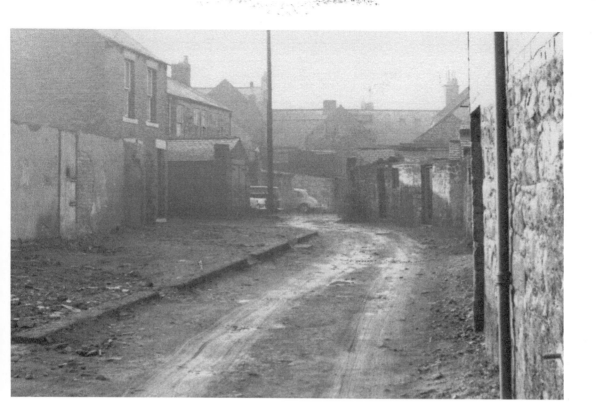

*F*awcett's Yard is named after Benjamin Fawcett, a veterinary surgeon who practised in the yard from 1868. It is seen in an appalling state in the older picture, which only dates back to around 1970.

After many years of neglect, the yard has been tidied up. The building on the right-hand side, nearest to Newgate Street, is Fawcett House, an old building that has been subject to much improvement over the years. Next to it is a rather younger building that is the home of the Physiotherapy and Sports Clinic, as well as consulting rooms used by the practice of

A. Cunningham and N. Clunies-Ross. There has been a physiotherapy business in the premises for some nineteen years. Prior to that the building was used as offices, having been adapted from a house by Davidson the builder in 1985. The building in the foreground on the left is much older, probably dating back to the eighteenth century. It is described on the next page.

*T*he early picture was taken at the start of the creation of the Back Riggs car park. The backs of the Manchester Street premises are seen clearly on the right along with Fawcett's Yard, behind the white car. The building with the slanting roof is easily identifiable as what is now the distinctive green-painted shop of Game Fishing Supplies. Prior to that it was occupied by T. & G. Interiors for a relatively short time, before which it was the Sports & Fishing shop. Whilst this part of the premises is not very old, the rest formed Nos 3 and 4 Fawcett's Yard, one up and one down cottages with outside toilets and a yard tap shown on the previous page. They were used as domestic dwellings without any substantial improvements until about the middle of the 1950s. To the west of the cottages, extending into what is now a small car park, there used to be a small stable and a hayloft.

7

Churches and Schools

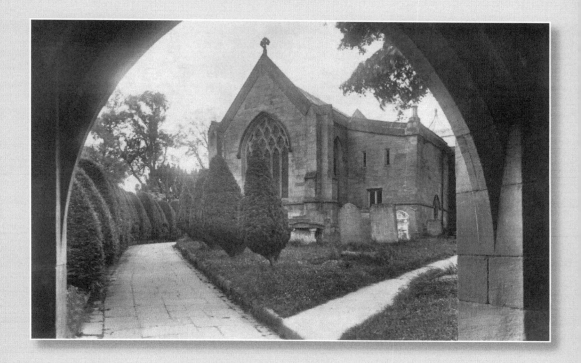

There are at least eight churches and at least eight schools in Morpeth. This chapter can only touch on some of them. The parish church of St Mary the Virgin, located on the southern approach road to the town and pictured here, is our oldest church. There was a chapel on the site in Anglo-Saxon times. The porch contains a list of incumbents, commencing with Helias in 1129 and continuing to the present day.

The church tower has a concave spire with a weather vane in the form of a fish. The different roof pitches of the chancel and the nave are thought to be due to the nave roof having been brought from the castle and recycled. The 'Jesse' window at the east end of the chancel is the most important fourteenth-century glass in the county and one of only five such windows in the country.

In 1842, the church contained high seats with canopies for the mayor and aldermen, as well as box pews and galleries. These were later removed by the Revd F.R. Grey to increase seating capacity to over 500.

This picture was taken at Newminster Abbey in 1914. It shows colonnades that were reconstructed during archaeological excavations at that time. The abbey was founded in 1138 by Ranulph de Merley, baron of Morpeth, on a site enclosed by a semi circle of hills. Eight Cistercian monks were sent from Fountains Abbey in Yorkshire to establish the abbey, which was dedicated to the Blessed Virgin Mary. The abbey was raided by the Scots on frequent occasions and visited by English kings going north to battle against them. After the Dissolution in 1537 the abbey buildings were destroyed and became a source of stone

for Morpethians until the nineteenth century. Very little stonework remains today, and the ruins stand on private land. The recent picture shows a rather neglected site, with the colonnades overgrown by hawthorn and brambles. Had the vandals of earlier centuries been kept at bay, Morpeth would have had a site of similar grandeur and importance as Fountains Abbey.

S t James' Church
was originally
surrounded by a high
and rather ugly red brick
boundary wall. In 1886
the churchyard was
extended northwards
to Copper Chare and a
splendid gateway was
erected to match the neo-
Norman-style church
designed by Benjamin
Ferrey, who had died in
1880. At the same time,
the brick wall was demolished and replaced by
the low stone wall that exists today.

This lychgate, under a Norman stone
archway, was a unique design at the time.
Unfortunately it has not survived. It had fallen
into a bad state of repair and was demolished
in around 1950. The gap in the stone wall
where the gateway stood is clearly visible in the
lower picture, showing the north entrance to
the church which was built in 1844-46.

The Wesleyan Methodist church on the north side of Manchester Street was built in 1884 to replace a chapel dating from before 1790. Built to seat a congregation of 400, it also had a schoolroom and vestry in the basement.

In 1932, the Wesleyan Methodists united with the Primitive Methodists and moved out to their church on Howard Road. The Morpeth Boys' Brigade took over the church building in 1964 for their parades and band practices, which had taken place previously in the parochial hall (the YMCA building in Dark Lane).

The eighteenth-century brick terrace house on the right of the church was called the

Wesleyan Rooms. This was the birthplace, in 1795, of Dr R. Blakey, who became a leader of the Chartist movement in the North East and a professor of logic and metaphysics at Queens College, Belfast. These houses were demolished in 1967, since when the site has been used as a car park. The Borough Council sold the land in 2004 for redevelopment as shops and flats.

The Primitive Methodist Church in Howard Road was built in 1904 to replace a smaller chapel in Manchester Street, where the Co-op funeral services business is today. The sloping site provided for the church to be built on the upper floor with a church hall below. The cost of £2000 was met by offerings and fundraising events. The Primitive Methodists and the Wesleyans were united in 1932 and shared the Howard Road church. In 1986 an extension was built on the east side to provide two meeting rooms, a new entrance hall, staircase and lift for the disabled in place of the external steps.

A millennium project was started in 2001, when the congregation began fundraising to revitalise the church and provide a centre for community service, based upon an impressive scheme of enlargement which was reduced by financial restriction. The building work began in September 2003 and was completed in June 2004. During this time the congregation shared services with St George's United Reformed Church.

The interior of the Methodist church is shown as it was built in 1904, with an arch over the stepped choir seating and the organ at the back. The view shows traditional church pews and a communion rail at the front.

The millennium project, completed in 2004, created space for the community centre and many improvements, including facilities for the disabled and a large lift. Chairs to allow a more flexible layout have now replaced the pews, while the choir seating has been removed to give a level floor with side-illuminated glazed screens stretching to the back wall. A new electronic organ has been installed at the side of the church, together with a new sound system and lighting.

*T*here has been a Presbyterian congregation in Morpeth since 1693. A chapel was built in Cottingwood Lane in 1721. It was extended later and remained in use until the present St George's Church opened beside the northern end of the Telford bridge in April 1860. The church had galleries on three sides and a rose window at the east end. However, in the late 1950s there was a need for a church hall and it was created above the original church by inserting a flat ceiling in the building to form a floor for the hall, a kitchen and a small meeting room. The alterations were completed in June 1963 at a cost of £16,500.

The clock on the church tower was presented by Mrs Mary Hollon in memory of her grandfather, the Revd Robert Trotter, who was minister from 1758 until 1807, and her uncle, Dr William Trotter, who was a Morpeth doctor and founded the Morpeth Dispensary. In 1970, the Presbyterian Church of England united with the Congregational Church to form the United Reformed Church

The grammar school was founded in around 1310 in the Chantry Chapel, where pupils were taught by the priests. It was re-founded by King Edward VI in 1552, remaining within the Chantry until 1846. It then operated from Harle House in Newgate Street until 1858, when a new building designed by Benjamin Ferrey was opened on the east side of Cottingwood Lane. The picture was taken in 1889 after extensions had been added, including an assembly hall, known as 'Big School'.

Successive Headmasters maintained high standards of discipline and academic achievement and developed sporting activities, leading to the need for an additional playing field in 1929. Northumberland County Council built a new school in 1967 on the old windmill field nearby. It was built to accommodate 530 grammar school boys and 500 high school girls, in separate buildings. The old grammar school buildings were demolished in 1971. Despite opposition, the schools became a comprehensive school in September 1973, known as King Edward VI School, to provide for 1420 pupils, including sixth formers.

St James' National School, as illustrated, was built in 1844 at the instigation of the Revd F.R. Grey, to provide religious and secular education for 330 pupils, with separate departments for boys and girls. The cost was met by grant aid and public subscriptions, including one from the founder, who also gave instruction. The school and its playground were built next to St James' Church. These buildings were later demolished to make a car park. In 1885, an infants school for 190 pupils was built on ground facing on to Wellway. This building is used today as the St James Community Centre.

In 1968 the main school was flooded by the Cottingburn and considerable damage was done, requiring the pupils to be evacuated into mobile classrooms. In 1972 the pupils were transferred to a new school built at Lancaster Park, designed to house 200 pupils and provided with a playing field and caretaker's house. Initially known as St Aidan's Church of England First School, it was renamed All Saints Church of England Aided School.

St Robert of Newminster Catholic First School is situated in Oldgate, next to Collingwood House. The lower picture shows the old school, built in 1850 at the same time as the church. In 1903 it became a voluntary aided school for the County Council and gradually enlarged with new classrooms. A dining hall was added in 1959.

These buildings were condemned by the Education Department in 1984 and after lengthy discussion were demolished in 1989 to allow a new school to be built on the site. The upper picture is of the new school, which was opened in 1991 by the Right Revd Owen Swindlehurst, Auxiliary Bishop of Hexham and Newcastle. The school comprises a hall, five classrooms and a nursery classroom and has facilities for 127 pupils. Over the main entrance there is a stained glass window depicting St Robert of Newminster, which had been found walled up in the presbytery opposite.

8

People

T here have been countless notable Morpethians and it is only possible to record a very few of them in this volume. Depicted on this page is Admiral Lord Collingwood, who was second in command to Nelson at the Battle of Trafalgar on 21 October 1805. He became commander-in-chief after Nelson was killed. Born in Newcastle in 1750, Collingwood was educated at the Royal Grammar School. He owned Collingwood House in Oldgate from 1791 until his death, at sea, in 1810.

Other notables, not covered in the following pages, include William Turner, the herbalist (1508-1568), painter Joseph Crawhall (born in Morpeth in 1861) and Robert Blakey (1795-1878), a tradesman and councillor who was mayor in 1836/37. Also born in Morpeth was Dr Morrison, who translated the *New Testament* into Chinese and compiled a Chinese dictionary.

The Hon. Revd Francis Richard Grey, MA (Cantab) was Rector of Morpeth from 1842 until he died in 1890. He was the sixth son of Earl Grey of Howick, and married Lady Elizabeth, daughter of the Earl of Carlisle. Influenced by the Oxford Movement, his 'High Church' ideas led to controversy about ritual. Parishioners wrote to complain to the bishop, leading to much correspondence.

On his appointment, the rector found the Church of St Mary to be a long way out of town and the Chantry Chapel condemned as unfit, and he was instrumental in the building of the Church of St James the Great in the town centre. It was opened by Lord Morpeth in October 1846, with fifty clergy in attendance and a civic reception afterwards. The cost of £7000 was met by public subscription. In 1887 the rector was presented with a golden chalice to mark fifty years of ministry.

The present rector is the Revd Robert McLean. Appointed by the Bishop of Newcastle in 2000, he administers to the three Anglican churches in the town.

*T*homas Burt was born in North Shields in 1837. He started work in the coalmines at the age of ten, becoming a hewer by the time he was eighteen. Having only a basic education, he taught himself by reading historical books and learned French, Latin and shorthand. At Choppington in 1860 he was appointed Secretary to the District Temperance Society. In 1865 he became Secretary to the Northumberland and Durham Miners Association.

He was elected MP for Morpeth in 1874 as a Liberal and the first working man to be an MP in Parliament. He was active in labour and social legislation and rose to be Secretary to the Board of Trade in 1892. In 1911 he received the honorary degree of Doctor of Civil Law from Durham University and the freedom of both Newcastle and Morpeth. He died in Newcastle in 1922.

The present MP for Wansbeck, which includes Morpeth, is Dennis Murphy, a Labour MP. He was elected to Parliament in 1997 after serving as Leader of Wansbeck District Council.

Williiam Strafford Sanderson was a trooper in the Boer War and a captain in the Durham Light Infantry during the First World War. He was five times mayor of Morpeth, serving for fifty-three years on the Council and on the County Council from 1919 to 1946. Mr. Sanderson advised on the purchase of Morpeth Town Hall from Lady Carlisle in 1915. He became an alderman in 1922, an Honorary Freeman in 1946 and was awarded the MBE in 1952. He died in 1973, aged ninety-three years.

Councillor Derek Thompson was mayor of Morpeth from 2003 to 2004, officiating at the reopening of Market Place after redevelopment works. He started work as a miner aged

fifteen at Lynemouth Colliery, trained in London as a teacher and taught in Kent before becoming headmaster at Stannington Hospital School in 1975. In 1982 he became headmaster at Gallowhill School, retiring in 1996. He was elected to the Town Council in 1995 and the Borough Council in 1998, and represents the Stobhill ward.

Miss Isobel Smail worked in the family shop on leaving school, volunteered in 1939 for service with the Northumberland Fusiliers and the Durham Light Infantry at Brancepeth Castle. She was later posted to Catterick with the Royal Corps of Signals. She is the granddaughter of John Smail, who came from Kelso in the 1890s to set up John Smail and Co. at No. 40 Bridge Street, selling ironware and numerous other goods. This emporium has served Morpethians ever since

and is now managed by the fourth generation of the family, helped by the fifth.

Miss Smail became a Town Councillor in 1964, and was a Borough Councillor for forty years, serving as mayor in 1971/72 and 1983/84. She was also on the Northumberland County Council for twelve years, being awarded the OBE in1995 and the freedom of Morpeth in 1996. Isobel was made an alderman in 1999 and a governor of King Edward VI School from 1973 to 2004. She is often to be found at the shop cash desk giving advice to customers.

*H*ere the 1918 Armistice Day parade marches down Bridge Street, led by the Town Mace Bearer, the mayor and the clerk to the Council followed by councillors and representatives of the armed services. The annual parade starts in the Market Place and then proceeds down Bridge Street, over the Telford bridge and up to the cenotaph. This war memorial, erected on a high mound above Mafeking Park, was built by public subscription and cost £1,200 to build. It shows the names of 232 men from the First World War and seventy-five men from the Second World War who lost their lives fighting.

A service of remembrance is held at the cenotaph, led by the rector and followed by wreath-laying by representatives from the Council, armed services and voluntary organisations. The parade then reassembles and is led back to the town hall.

In 2004 a parade was held to award the freedom of Northumberland to HMS Northumberland, led by their colour party.

*T*he man in the bowler hat was Jack Dixon, who was a town crier and bellman employed by the Town Council on market days to announce the start and closing times of trading. He is seen with his 'scout', Mitford, in the market in 1894. The last bellman was Norman Froud, caretaker at the town hall.

Shown in the lower photograph is the 'Morpeth Gadgy', created in 1968 to represent the old town bailiffs. He presides at gathering festivities and special events, including the reopening of Market Place in 2003. Alex Swailes has been the 'Gadgy' for the last eight years. A former headmaster and JP for over thirty years, he founded the Morpeth Operatic Society in 1962 and is well known as an after-dinner speaker on matters Northumbrian. He was made an MBE in the 2005 New Years Honours List for services to the community.

A trip into the country has always sounded like a good idea – and a lucrative opportunity for coach operators. Miss Micah Elliott was one of Morpeth's characters. She had a general dealers shop in Oldgate that maintained its Victorian appearance until the day it closed in 1986, by which time Miss Elliott was well into her eighties. In 1911 she was living at No. 25 Oldgate and advertising her twenty-seater charabanc for hire. Alec Tweddle's *Town Trails* tell us that the vehicle was used as a wagon during the week but that at weekends benches were placed across it for seats. Tweddle also indicates that Miss Elliott drove it herself on occasion.

The modern picture shows the Morpeth Antiquarian Society outing to Fountains Abbey in July 2004. One suspects that the journey was more comfortable than it might have been in 1911. Whilst the lack of a roof on the charabanc influenced what people wore, the lack of formality in 2004 is very striking.

Frederick Schofield was mayor of Morpeth in 1889/90 and a councillor for eleven years. He was also organist at St George's Church from 1880 to 1907. Trained in London as a dispensing chemist, he bought the Newgate Street business now known as Sim & Webb in 1877. As well as dispensing prescriptions for local doctors Mr Schofield dispensed medicines for both domestic and farm animals and appears to have been known far

beyond Morpeth for his skills in that direction. A successful breeder and exhibitor of both dogs and poultry, he was in demand as a judge at agricultural shows. In 1897, Mr Schofield was living at No. 12 Castle Square. He moved to The Retreat in Dark Lane, which was later to become the home of Geoff Brown, the vet, and is now vacant. The current pharmacist at Sim & Webb is Mr R. Black. It is interesting to compare the style of dress used now with that of 100 years ago.

The lower picture was taken in about 1932 to mark the launch of a new-model Ford 8. It cost £100. The tall gentleman behind the three children on the left of the picture is George Young, company secretary of Jennings at the time. Standing on his own in front of the car is Bob Mills, foreman at Ford Cars, and on his left in light coloured trousers is Walter Craigs, who was in the sales department. Next but one to him, in plus fours, is Jack

Batey, who was on the agricultural side of the business. The identity of the distinguished looking couple at the front of the car is not known.

Today's premises are at Coopies Lane industrial estate and the upper picture shows the modern glass-fronted showroom, with sales staff on the forecourt. Mr A. Bentley is the Managing director of this Ford agency

Jim Alder was born in Glasgow to an Irish father and a Scottish mother. He settled in Morpeth at the age of nine and was to become a famous runner. Between the ages of twenty and forty he ran over 100,000 miles. Jim is pictured in the 1976 Great North Run, flying through Stannington at such speed that both feet are off the ground. Today he does not fly so fast, but remains active by helping to train the younger members of the Morpeth Harriers.

In 1966 Jim won a gold

medal for the marathon, as well as a bronze medal for the 10,000 metres event in the Commonwealth Games in Jamaica. In 1969 he took the bronze medal for the marathon at the European Games in Athens, and 1970 saw him win a silver medal for the marathon at the Commonwealth Games in Edinburgh. In addition, Jim held several world records as well as sixty-nine medals in track and cross-country events in Northumberland and Durham.

The Morpeth Harriers were formed in 1947 at the Greyhound Inn on Newgate Street, where their meetings were held. The lower picture, taken in 1949, shows club members assembled outside the inn. The current club president, Ernie Slaughter, is in the back row, fifth from the right. In the 1950s the club moved to Grange House field, and they moved into the present clubhouse (adjoining Morpeth Rugby Club) in 1968. From a modest start membership has risen to over 300 and it is now one of the top running clubs in the country, regularly winning medals in national championships. Over the years the club has produced international competitors at various levels, including Jim Alder and Mark Hudspith, a bronze medallist at the Edmonton Commonwealth Games in 1994.

The Harriers compete in a wide range of athletic events for all ages, taking part in road racing, cross country, fell running and orienteering events. The upper picture shows the road relay bronze medallists at Sutton Coldfield in 1999.